In Silence

ENIGMA

To depression, anxiety, and the consistent efforts
of staying a few steps ahead
of the least appreciated parts of us.

To overriding the undercurrent,
to having faith while sometimes not even having
as much as a clue.

To going beyond presumed possibilities.
This is to choosing love, every time,
over and over and over again.

CONTENTS

To:

Cheryl Andrea Sebro,
No acknowledgement could possibly convey my level of
gratitude for your contribution to this book or to me as
your son. From the deepest parts of me, thank you.
I love you.

&

Myrtle Evangeline Scope,
You are and always have been my lighthouse. The Creator
hears your name and the thanks I pour out for the
overabundance of gifts I have been blessed with in you.
You had and will always have all of the love I am able to
give.

Thank you.

FROM UNDER THEIR BREATH

<u>Impediment</u>

Intricacy once found in their order
Interrupted by an unwelcome stammer
A vicious cycle at inception
Fated to a downward spiral
A stumble, minuscule and unassuming
Trendsetting
Rippling the water
Leaving a wake of jumbled sentiments
Silence, the destination

<u>Grand Gestures</u>

I want to be
Wrapped up in the tiny things

Like time

And love

And

You

<u>Bonfire</u>

I was envious of her harnessed freedom
She grasped it tightly
Wrung it between her fingers
Squeezed every bit of it out of its own bondage
And danced
Bound herself to a rhythm
Rode the waves of melodies
Rolling against the cadence
Imposed her curvature into the atmosphere
Became a welcomed occupant
Took time
Space
The attention at which I stood
And danced
Called for response with movement
But I was frozen
Entranced by her authenticity
Stuck but being set ablaze in this incidence
She was incendiary
Desire swelled to the right of everything I'd left behind
And she danced
Beckoning for someone to join her
Too enamored to move
Too mesmerized to choose
I was lost
In the bends of her groove

<u>Maybe</u>

Maybe
I already was and just didn't know it
Or I knew and
Didn't want to admit it
Maybe
Intensity should have scared me and
Just didn't
Or
It did and my togetherness
Was a front
Maybe
I was enthralled
Totally encompassed
Completely engulfed
Maybe
That was infatuation
Maybe
My need to be felt would
Combine with your need to be touched
And we'd ride the current
Or
We'd kiss and
Be set adrift on a sea of possibilities
Disregard everything that doesn't affect us
Or we'll pretend that
This isn't what it just might be and
The surprise wouldn't settle in so shockingly because
Maybe
You already were and just didn't know it
Or
You knew and felt you couldn't show it
But you can
You can
You can

<u>Untitled | 05.26.16</u>

He held her head in his hands
Had his way with her lips
She heard him clearly
Kisses, like alarms
Urgency
Absolutely
Undeniable

AT A DEPTH BEYOND COMPREHENSION

Aging Disgracefully

He wore resented phrases on his brow
Old feelings took hold of faint marionette lines
His inability to conceal – effortlessly revealing

<u>Rolling Stone</u>

Brown cascaded from bottle to tumbler
He dreamt out of sequence
In portions and pieces that abandoned their order
Mimicking his predisposition to assert himself
He sipped slowly
In contrast to racing thoughts
No end in sight or sound
Freedom clanging annoyingly amongst the chaos
Drum patterns pattering
Pity-less and against his wishes
Gone
A slave to obsessions at the close of day
They paced effortlessly through his mind
With pronounced gaits and irresistible expressions
His past returned clearly every evening
Dusk giving the demons the clear
He sipped slowly
Motionless between swigs
Oak-barrel-brown warming him from within
Each a silent attempt to quell their snarls
To hush their snickers
To drown them back into submission
Futile
Painful nostalgia on his chest
As he swallowed aged fire and held on
In no rush to leave
No one to go home to
No one to call for company
Empty
Murmured for more through a crooked smile
· Just a while turning into much longer
Mumbling about old memories
Past lovers
Once a stone's throw away
Now distant

When The Signal Fades

Admittedly
I am unsure, somewhat embarrassed
But too unashamedly honest to be anything other than
whom I've always been
This has been my least favorite part since the very first
time
I resolve to believe the fallacy that I let you leave when
In truth
Your departure was never in my control
No tire tracks or burnt rubber
No rush to move on
The shadows of your presence linger long after you've
gone
Making your absence so much more than simply a void
I can still feel you through the static of distance
Too far away yet it seems that you're here still
Up against the seams
Here, still
Pushing
Your effect always seems to be everlasting
There are complications, now
A slight shudder
Jumbled-word-dribble-formation
A stutter while whispering your name
Pacing slowly away from the last place I will have seen you
Until the next time
While I'm here
Fuck time
In all of its relativity
Too short to be not long enough to miss you the way I do
So damn long that I can't help but to
I can still feel you through the static of distance
Without the placing of blame
Without ascribing to any semblance of guilt
I acknowledge that it's unfair

Make futile attempts to stare out of disappointment
Peer into the half-baked idea that you feel half as strongly
as I do
Appear lost in fantasy
Imagine that you'd have me
If you could
Equally as much as I could have you
Always
In all ways
Intellectually, first
Sexually, secondly
When the signal fades I resort to roaming the halls in my
head
Crowded with memories of days that have yet to happen
Pictures of perfectly placed hands about your body
PDA in various locations
Vacations
Staycations
Days of doing absolutely nothing
Just what we need
Conversations of revolution
The resolution to end in orgasm every other time
Because either I or we
I'm not sure which yet
Can't seem to keep hands off
And with all of this
I can feel you through the static of distance, still

Distilled Confession

The answers
Never hid themselves
At the bottom of bottles
But brown spirits brought me
Temporary freedom while
The answers
Kept me in contempt

Tactile

Calloused hands told the stories
Kept in the deepest dark
Sent details
Tumbling into view with every greeting
With every handshake
Every "Nice to meet you…"
He was rough with his hands
Rough in his ways
Rough in days past
And shame would whisper his name
As he reached for reasons
Holding back bloody-knuckle memories
Reaching out for reasons
Palm-down
Pushing up memories
He had a working man's hands
Ones that held tightly
Hurled and twisted when necessary
Hands that swelled when abused
Cramped
Cracked
Lurched forward on command
Ones that held tightly
Yearned to be held… tightly
Ugly and capable
Thick hands
With thick fingers that mocked the thick of things
That mocked everything he'd been through
They knew all of his secrets
Told a few
Echoed his damage in broken skin
Broken in
Calloused hands that craved attention
That missed everything they haven't had
Lonely

Left to swing in the wind
To nurse their own wounds
Longing to be anything other than
Left alone
He had strong hands
They had no other option but to be
Constantly grasping at the breeze
Quietly clawing at hope
Still soft where hardening should be
Battered hands
Denied their simple desire
Reaching for relief
Regrets gathered at his fingertips
Nothing hidden
Hands that held tightly
Hoping to love and be loved
And be held… Tightly
Calloused hands
Waiting patiently

Sarcasm

Lie to me like I begged you to
Make it all seem true
I yearn to hold an ill-gotten smile

<u>In The Wake Of You</u>

Sometimes, your departure still feels fresh
Love, you were cradled by failure in ways no one could
prepare for
Time was of no significance
Around you, temporary madness revolved
Glorious uncertainty demanded attention
I was swallowed whole in your development
To have and hold
An impossibility by second trimester
Love, you had come
Cast ripples, shaken peace to pieces, and gone
Some nights now
Crimson tides call me from slumber
I remember you in guilt
Fault never tries hard
Finds me feigning pleasure in the wake of you
In the dark I ponder your looks
How deeply your brow would furrow
Which side of your smile would remain static
The sound of your cry
Color of your skin, your eyes
The unsteady elegance in your gait
I consider all you could have been
What you wouldn't
Quirks we would have laughed over
Qualms we would have fought under
Similarities, differences, moments of perfection
The days, the ways I should be discovering to say that I
love you
Today, your departure still feels fresh

WHEN THE UNIVERSE
GOES STILL

In Closing

I remember praying from a broken place
That was the night before last
Flying at half-mast after being told
I would never be good enough
The night before the last for me
This will not hurt
A sleep unlike any other
I could have smothered myself with empty reassurance

I just wanted to breathe

Freedom came in capsule form
And I swallowed it by the fist-full
Flying at half-mast after being told
I would never be good enough
No blaze of glory
No meaningful outro
No accentuated exit

I just wanted to breathe

<u>Be Gentle</u>

Take your transgressions
Fold them neatly
And cast them into the wind
You are not the mistakes you've made

<u>Beckon</u>

Cocoon me in your love
Carry me through the very metamorphosis you call for us
to come through to get back to you
With your unwavering angst, draw me ever nearer
Cast down even any conspiracy for my failure
Keep me close
Steady my gait
Order my steps
Coax me in your direction and impress upon me the
necessity to be in your likeness
To spite the way of life that continually loosens us from
your hold
The very way that keeps us captive
Capture my essence and wrap it up in your glory
Pour me blessing after blessing in abundance
Remain open to my call, receptive to my beckoning
Arm me
As a soldier of your word and in your light that I may
stand, unfaltering
Be with me forever
And into infinity
Ase, Ase, Ase

<u>Now and Then</u>

I visit every now and then
Pull you from the archives and
Remember the times after we'd broken
And were falling into each other again
What wasted efforts we'd put forth
Pacing the halls of each other's beings
Occupying spaces we had no business being
Simply being
The growth was minimal there
I smile now when I think of you
First, because I think of you
Then because there always seems to be
Some absurdity that comes with retaining memories of you
My dentist says I should stop grinding my teeth
That I need enamel for protection but
He never understands when I tell him you're in my Scope
That I can't seem to wash the taste of you from my mouth
That brushing is an act in futility
That mint-flavored floss
Doesn't quite cut through your plaque
That you're a plague I can't seem to get rid of
You show up every now and then
Unpack yourself and park in the center
Demand attention you should no longer have command
over
What wasted efforts you put forth
Pacing the halls of my being
Occupying spaces you have no business being
Simply being
I smile now when I think of you
First, because I think of you
Then, because I'm pushing away the memories of you
Even if the effect is only temporary

Shadow Boxing

There's that feeling again

Like… drowning

Like the most infamous memory in the light of nostalgia
A most succulent sorrow
Swollen with indignation

Like… drowning

<u>Obsolete</u>

I suppose
What we had then in comparison to what we have now
was too great
And you finally got tired of living in what you described as
this prison
You sought out your sovereignty
And I'm thankful
Because really, you freed me from a cage I didn't even see
being built around me
Your vision was always a bit better than mine anyway
At first, it seemed unbearably premature
The way you left
Entirely too soon
I'd grown accustomed to the sweetness of drowning in you
To the ease of losing myself
In the monotony of days gone by
To the repetition of hello's and goodbye's
Laced with the caress of your lips
We once existed in a state of reckless disregard
And the guards that sometimes seem to be set in stone
Didn't always have a home, here
We colored outside of each other's lines
Adoration was our Adderall
And nightfall would witness our sins
But eventually

The version of me you fell in love with wasn't enough
anymore

You professed your love and
Later buried your proclamation
Scaled back and hid away
Teased me with your delicacy and
Left me lonely in my persistence
You left me alone in a once shared existence

Naked and vulnerable

You commanded my mind
Demanded that my lust awaken at will and
Stretch and rise and swell especially for you
You wrung me dry and left me thirsting
Swooning over your leftover scent
Reaching for your shadow
Sifting through wishes which would never come true
You would never come through
You would never stay
You would say lots of things
None of which would manifest
All of which would go just as soon as you left
And I'm thankful now
Embracing what I refused to
I'm accepting that I won't change you
That you won't change
That things won't change
That we've gone too far out of range
There's no signal
And regardless of my perception
With you
I'm no longer well received

THE GATEWAY DRUG
THAT LED TO THIS

<u>Somehow</u>

You make
Existing
Without contact
Seem like
A punishment
Both cruel
And unusual
Quietly, you
Convert it to
A requisite
Regularly met
With resistance
Plotted against
Constantly
Somehow
You've managed
To maneuver
The loner
From his
Perpetual desire
For solitude

<u>Have Your Way</u>

Have your way
Take me by the nape of my neck and
Coax me
Push me south of the only border that ever mattered
Demand that I drive you insane
Try to remain composed
But I want to expose that beast inside of you
Lover
I'm determined to dig up every reservation you've ever
retained
More than ready to risk my last breath
In attempts to breach the bounds of the octaves of your
voice
Come to rest on my thighs
Then shoulders
Allow that arch to rise
And push that prize my way
Whisper every thing you've never said aloud
It's all allowed here
Be loud and clear
Scream as I squeeze you
And sip your nectar
Thirsty for your truths
For the climaxes of your reality
I present my purpose orally
Orchestrate you into euphoria
Exercise my strongest muscle
Stretch you wide
Rub you down from inside
Slide the tip
From the top
Lightly over
With fervor between
Noting every tone in which you scream
Changing directions on command

27

ENIGMA

Watching you unravel
Reveling in your pleasure
Licking and sticking rhythmically
Commanding
Leave me scratched
Reach for everything and nothing
Release with resolve
I dare you
Drown me
Lover
Have your way

<u>Captive</u>

You command my mind
Demand my lust awaken from its slumber
Stretch and rise and swell
With a yearning especially for you
You wring me and leave me thirsting
Alone and swooning over your leftover scent
Reaching for your shadow
Sifting through wishes
All of which will come true
You come through
A violent wind
Gale-forced
You stroke the most vivid memories
You provoke me
Your every gust begs me
To come
And stay

Relinquish

Let me pass over your pulse
Ensure you're still here
Discover stillness and permit me
Palms up
Wince and purr at
Points of pressure pressed against
React unknowingly
Pull me close
And promise not to push me
Huff away caution in labored breaths
Strip free of apprehension
Ascend on the lift of my lips
Come to climax as I speak in tongue
Let me pass over your pulse
Ensure you're still here
Snatch you from where I've taken you
Set you easy
Rest you quietly
In the calm called after your showers

<u>Early</u>

Morning
The undone darkness
Rousing a reaction to your absence
I desire you, early
Well before the world's risen
Daybreak
A well-placed pedestal
For moans
Whimpers
Whispers
Smiles

She

Blessed was she
With cup lines
Like fault lines that
Converge at the perimeter
The perineum
Where near-earth-quaking cadences are played on Richter's
scale
Title-chanting tidal waves
Rush from spring
Tucked away tightly in
What could only be laborious glory
I imagine her being shaped between index and thumb
To the rhythm of Motherland drum patterns
Broadcasted live from
The furthest of Saturn's rings
Her curvature singing in the soprano-tone of
Ethereal ethnicity
A Siren's song
Ringing alarms no one could sleep through
Attention sequestered in God-breathed existence
And he is gifted with her concern
Eagerly cocooned in the space
Where her croons might otherwise
Roam freely
She commands him
Copulate the very place once taken
In the time of her tonsil's tenure
Her willing endurance enticing an eruption
Murmurs massaging a new member in the most
Unapologetic candor
Calling celebratory exaltations
Forcing former beliefs to be recanted
But this isn't so much worship
As it is sin

<u>She Called Him</u>

He sought out synonyms for soft in efforts to describe her
Attempted to find the proper words
Like Rights of passage
Like deciphering foreign tongues
Like navigating uncharted territory
Like prerequisites for penning the perfect description
She was an untold story
Carried the antiquity of an old wise tale
While still presenting as new
And being packaged beautifully

Plush

Mildly expressive but sensitive to artistry
He imagined parables resting on her tongue
Awaiting moments of pristine imperfection
To be rambled off in soft whispered tones
Low on purpose
As to afford that blessing to only those who listened
On purpose
He was always listening
There was something
Homely and familiar
And he loved it when she called him Black Man
Maybe it was the abundant satisfaction
Peeking through her vocal upswing as she sang the phrase

Or the way it yanked him from the past

<u>Non-verbal</u>

I couldn't recant if I wanted to
Seduction poured from her pores
She had me ensnared
This... was unfair
I struggled to hold my bearings
But
She touched me
Again
And I knew, this was awkward
This was new
Assured her that she could do whatever she wanted to do
That compliance was all she needed to rely upon
That there were no signs of defiance
I was all in
Her fingers bent
Twisted into mine and time
Lost its significance
This... This was not sex
This... was conversation
Skin collided with skin
Rippled feelings sent like waves
Racing up extremities
The extent of the damage, unknown
But I'd break
And be broken repeatedly
If it meant we could touch
Again and again and again
She reeled backwards
Retracted but called me closer still
I was a constant mess
Maddened by the yearning to be
The focus of her full potential
I could see
It lurked beneath her unassuming surface
She could give birth

IN SILENCE

To a burst of constant energy
She could overwhelm me
I wanted to promise not to resist
But I couldn't speak when she touched me
When we touched, we
Connected
She cringed as I passed over areas of sensitivity
Upper waist
Neck
Inner thigh
We spoke each other's language fluently
Fluidly we fluctuated
Emphasis on hers
Then mine
Lost in a rift of time
She was modest
And I understood
Honestly... I didn't care for what scared her
Because fear was a figment
That covered everything that could be
Everything we could be
She pinned me
I sinned internally but it was only momentarily
She attracted me
Was my polar opposite with almost too many similarities
Chemistry was our major
Allowed me the privilege to pass over places
Forbidden previously
Smiled a half-smile
She reacted physically
We were without interruption
Disregarded every disruption
Lost in fantasy
Satisfying the cravings
But this... This was not sex
This... was conversation
This... was communication

Four And A Half Steps

You know
They whispered under their breath about you
Tested their abilities to whisper... or not to
As you walked by
Stepping... so... strongly towards wherever we were going
Places that never seemed to matter as long as you never
saw
What I was showing
Speaking only boldly enough to impress myself

From a perfect... four and a half of a step... behind

Too many for you to realize
But far enough for me to theorize all about you and
Not those jeans... or the means by which I could
Obtain you
If even for just a while
Instead, if poetry or prose would persuade you
Ways on top of ways to invade... your mind
How to find that link to bind myself to yours

All from a perfect... four and a half of a step... away

Just far enough to theorize while not distorting my view
Trudging forward through the aftermath of your silent
Invisible and still tangible grandeur
I'd quietly wonder whether or not your weather ever
changed
If maybe you were... different at night
If that blackened shell broke away
To show the sweet meat that you refuse to let get beat
By the street, by life, by death, by drama, by trouble, by all
things unfortunate
By the heat... of reality
I'd quietly wonder if you were... softer

IN SILENCE

More heartfelt
The opposite of that tough exterior
All that as they whispered under their breath about you
Speaking sentences slathered with obscenities and
Every un-verbalized fantasy you never knew I had about
you
Every single thing I dare not say
But couldn't bring myself to stay away from
And every once in a while you'd turn
Look my way and smile
Reaching ever closer to our destination
And by my approximation moments like this almost
Couldn't get any better
And by my estimation it was another of the sweetest of the
sweet

Only four and a half steps

From taking a step in ill-preparation
Stepping up to step away form the nirvana
Only experienced in my fantasies
One step beneath ecstasy
A step from talking to you
Telling you everything and nothing that I don't normally
tell you
Because we've spoken, so it wouldn't be the first time
But that time that step would be different so I

Stayed those four and a half steps away

Where I could boldly speak to myself
And listen
As they whispered under their breath about you

<u>One More Time</u>

I deny my flight response

Like a fool, I want it so badly I abandon it

I charge forward into a future that refuses to reveal itself
until it's too late

There's a new someone

They draw from stilled waters and pull at strings gone
untouched for too long
They cast light on the days that lack.
They call that feeling up and out of me

It takes a seat on my diaphragm; leans against my sternum
and the moments I live for manifest
It lacks a name, which doesn't really matter and that fear
has since begun phasing itself in

I suppose I could rush back into seclusion — back into
security, but I want what scares me

Like a fool, I charge forward

I hope I float
I hope I never hit the ground, but if I do — I hope it
doesn't hurt too badly to get up and try one more time

Untitled | 06.19.16

I still smell you in my space
It's as if you're still here
The scent of coconut and quiet passion

I shut my eyes in attempts to recreate you
Piece together brown sugar sweetened memories
Find a melody to manifest you by
And mantra the ways I can't wait to have you

Softened curves casing slender frame
Arrive in silence
Light touches call for imaginary riot
Rouse the rebel within
Send me into a frenzy
Keeping calm quickly becoming a casualty
To your allure

You're like a scoop of hellfire

Standing just close enough
Present and warm
Inviting in the most hypnotizing way
Freezing me in place
Holding my gaze
Kindling my embers
Attempting to set me ablaze

And I allow you

Eyes held shut as not to lose you
You become a dream
While having you is deferred by distance
While I wonder

Why not fix this

ENIGMA

Why not get closer
I stay far enough away to remember
What the cold feels like
Far enough away to reminisce
Humming hymnals about your heat
Far enough away for desire to haunt me
For your whispers to echo
For me to reach without touching

And I want to

I stay far enough away to see if you will
Reach for me
Far enough away to recognize reciprocation
I remain in your orbit
Lie in wait
Take risk
Give you license to waste my time
I keep my eyes closed and blow kisses to memories
Hope they'll return fire
Hope you'll return and replenish me

I mantra the ways that I wait to have you

Behind a found melody to manifest by
Attempt to recreate you
I'm called to action
By remnants of coconut and quiet passion
I'm called to action

By the residue of you

BUT A BIGGER SIN
TO NOT BE SHAKEN

Instinct

Unfortunately
This place is a familiar one
We clamor at open windows
About-faced to every closed door
Sanctifying any ground we find ourselves standing on
Solid, and fertile with opportunities for movement
To settle would also be to blaspheme
We could rest on just what they tell us to be
Each a carbon copy
Destined to be detoured into a shallow grave
Just deep enough for only the potential we chose to use
We could be
Silent
Reverent
In full compliance
Within the bounds of mindless obedience
In close proximity to empty promises

But to be free

Calls out to us in sync with our suppressed melodies
Conjures the rhythms and begs that we be
To our highest degree
The desire digs at our insides
Do you feel it
Demanding that we break out
Demanding that we live
As death threatens from the shadows

The yearning to be free mantras outwardly from our
centers

We emanate the energy of our possibilities
We embody greatness in potential
Born of decisions to persist

IN SILENCE

Each of us
Love's children conceived in chaos
Cradled in the warmth of our ancestors disobedience

The desire to be free

Resides not on the outskirts
But just beneath the surface
Feel it
There
The beckon and call to be nothing less than our fullest
selves
To be unmoving and steady
To be steadfast and headstrong

The desire to be free

Humming like a hymnal in the depths of our minds
In the lowest of frequencies
Resonating within our bones
Sanctifying any ground we find ourselves standing on
Solid, and fertile with opportunities for movement
Our foot bottoms
Stained red with ancestral passion
This inheritance an ember we only have to kindle
A call which
To be free

We only have to answer

<u>Zombies</u>

I saw them all

Baldwin. Lorde. Du Bois. Baraka. Garvey. Hughes.
Hurston. Thurston. Kuti. Morrison. Davis. Patterson.
Newton. Shakur. X. Anderson. Bland. Rice. Boyd. Brown.
Martin.

I heard them
I couldn't sleep

The shots haunted me in my awake-state
And I could only contemplate
What if he, were me
When does enough
Become too much to stomach
WAKE UP
Every sleeping body
Somebody wake up
Every
Sleeping
Body
There's a war outside
And we're hibernating
Damned to a hellish existence
With the devil's assistance in terror
We should never have been taken

But the bigger sin is to not be shaken

No

Be shaken

Awaken and rise
Answer to the wails of innocence emanating from the

earth like an alarm
We exist with the fantasy of safety
They hate us down to the way we walk
And the way we breathe
It seems they can't conceive a world where we receive
equality
So systematically they strip us of our life
Tease us with tasers
Gun us down in the streets
And I couldn't sleep
I would blame it on a nightmare
But reality kept me questioning
How exactly could this be
WAKE UP
Every sleeping body
Somebody wake up
Every
Sleeping
Body
To appeal to their morality becomes an impossibility
The heartless have no conscience
We have to be conscious
This IS about us
Don't believe differently
WAKE UP
Wake Up
wake up

<u>We Carry The Burden</u>

We
Inherited the struggle of our ancestors
The struggle of our great grandparents
The struggle of momma and daddy
We inherited the struggle
We took without option
The blood's been spilled
In the name of Blackness
Because we're Haitian by association
Because we're 4 million Brazilians never repatriated
Because we're Creole and Geechee and from the South
But furthest from dirty
We are well beyond belief
Because we inhabit both hemispheres
Because we hold history in our bones
We possess the power to produce variation regardless of
variables
We are the source point
The beginning
The ones who started it all
We cradle stories on our tongues
Tuck them away
Within life and death's defining line
And make them come alive
We open our mouths and allow them
That which we've been denied
Freedom
We've been denied just the same as they were
Because we inherited the struggle of our ancestors
So we reach for higher heights
We came upon the obligation
To make our own way
To create ripples in reservoirs not reserved for us
To both stake out and take hold of a status quo
That at times doesn't even count us

We came upon the obligation
To continue demanding to be seen as we are
As we always have been
As human
We took the brunt of the weight
In transfer from beaten backs
To youthful shoulders
Now we uphold and define
Now we're at the beck and call of those who've fallen
Because we're Trans-Atlantic travelers
Because we're 18th century Black Nova Scotians
Because we're nearly every bit of the Caribbean
Because we're rhythm
And effortless melody
And the literal depiction of God
Can be found in each of our bodies
We inherited the struggle of our ancestors
We took without option
The struggle of our great grandparents
And by existing we've secured our place
We take up spaces and the world trembles
At the sight of our faces
And the world shudders at every one of our steps
And the world stutters in attempts to answer back
With No good excuses for the abuse
Like a child born to privilege
Typical
While with no choice
We take the immense weight of our legacies
We were born sun-kissed
The untamable offspring of the ultimate lover
Creation's children
Bold enough to do anything we set our minds to
Born royalty in the midst of trouble
We fell into the center of responsibility
We carry the burden now
We carry the burden

Write to express; not impress.

THANK YOU

Myrtle Evangeline Scope.
Pearl Bowie-Harmon.
Norma Altidor.
Miguel Casimir.
Rachelle Faublas.
Richard "Byrd" Wilson.
Adrian "Lovebook" Carter.
Sharonda "Eccentrich" Chery.
Suneeta "Sunni Da Poet" Williams.
Rebecca "Butterfly" Vaughns.
Calvin "Made S.O.N." Early.

You each in your own way have played an integral part in the creation and assembly of this body of work.

The Nuyorican Poets Café.

Thank you for showing your love to a teenager who had never read his poetry aloud to anyone before.

The South Florida poetry scene.

Thank you for fostering art in its various forms and for inspiring me, continually, throughout this process and for everyone who has ever given me a thought or word of encouragement.

Made in the USA
Middletown, DE
16 September 2021